# COULD BE
# AND SHOULD BE

## UNLOCKING YOUR INNER STRENGTH

# COULD BE
## AND SHOULD BE

**UNLOCKING YOUR INNER STRENGTH**

**A JOURNEY OF SELF-DISCOVERY,
RESILIENCE, AND TRANSFORMATION**

**DR. DOTUN OYEWOLE**

PHOS
PUBLISHING.LLC

**Could Be and Should Be, Unlocking Your Inner Strength**

2023 © Dr. Dotun Oyewole

First Edition: 2023

ISBN: 979-8-9889364-0-4 (Paperback)
ISBN: 979-8-9889364-1-1 (eBook)
ISBN: 979-8-9889364-2-8 (Hardcover)

Library of Congress Control Number: 2023915624

Unless otherwise noted, scripture quotations are from the King James Version. Quotations marked "NKJV" are from the New King James Version®. Copyright ©1982 by Thomas Nelson. Used by permission. All rights reserved.

Editing by Jessica Hatch, Hatch Editorial Services, LLC

Cover and interior design by Becky's Graphic Design®, LLC, www.BeckysGraphicDesign.com

To the Almighty God, the fountain of inspiration,
strength, guidance, and the answer to all mysteries,
this book is humbly dedicated.

# Table of Contents

**10** Transitioning from the Known to the Unknown

Acknowledgments

About the Author

Leave a Review

# The Revelation of Possibility

*Discovering the Known and the Unknown*

In the realm of personal growth and self-discovery, extraordinary moments have the power to ignite a profound transformation. Such a moment unfolded in my life on a fateful morning—Saturday, November 18, 2006. In a vision, the Lord appeared to me, assuming the form of one of my college professors—an English professor. With authority and clarity, he approached the board, taking up the chalk, and inscribed a statement that would forever shape my understanding: "Just as in mathematics, when solving word problems, we assign variables to the known and find the unknown. Our topic today is 'Could Be and Should Be.'"

Startled awake, I found myself captivated by these enigmatic words. They resonated deep within me, awakening a relentless curiosity that would guide my path for years to come. Two burning questions took root within my soul, demanding answers:

- What does the known represent?
- What lies within the realm of the unknown?

For nearly seven years, I pondered these questions, seeking the elusive truth that lay hidden beneath their surface. Then, on a momentous day—March 24, 2013—the Lord unveiled the answers I had yearned for.

In the pages that follow, I invite you to join me on an extraordinary journey of self-discovery and personal transformation. Together, we will explore the profound concepts of the known and the unknown, unraveling their mysteries and unlocking the vast potential they hold within our lives.

This self-help book is not a mere collection of theoretical ideas or empty promises. It is a testament to the power of revelation and the unwavering guidance of a higher power. Through my own experiences and encounters, I will share with you the invaluable lessons I have learned—lessons that have the potential to illuminate your path, inspire your actions, and empower you to embrace a life of purpose and fulfillment.

As we embark on this adventure, I encourage you to approach each page with an open heart and a receptive mind. Engage in reflective introspection, allowing the words to penetrate your being and awaken the dormant possibilities within you. Pause and pray when a particular insight resonates deeply, for it is in these sacred moments that the Divine reveals Himself in extraordinary ways.

The revelation of possibility awaits you. Let us embark together, navigating the intricacies of the known and the unknown, and uncovering the transformative truths that lie within. May this journey be a catalyst for your personal growth, igniting the flame of hope and guiding you toward a future filled with purpose, clarity, and unwavering certainty.

# CHAPTER ONE

# A Journey Beyond Boundaries

*Unleashing My Extraordinary Potential*

Welcome to the captivating pages of my self-help book, where the flames of inspiration are kindled and the embers of greatness glow within you. Prepare to embark on a transformative expedition through the realms of perseverance, faith, and self-discovery. Brace yourself for a tale that will reshape your thoughts, ignite your spirit, and guide you toward a life of fulfillment and boundless possibilities.

## Embracing the Inner Prodding

Close your eyes and envision me as a young boy in rural Africa, my footsteps echoing against the backdrop of struggle. Picture my family, grappling with the bitter reality of scarcity, where even three square meals a day seem like an unattainable dream and the persistent specter of unpaid school fees looming over my siblings and me was a familiar symphony. Yet, amid the adversities, a gentle nudge deep within my soul ignites a belief in me, an unwavering conviction that I am destined for greatness beyond ordinary imagination. I dared to defy circumstances, envisioning a life that transcended these limitations. Little did I know that this inner prodding would set in motion an extraordinary odyssey.

## Discovering the Power of Vision

Travel back in time with me to the tender age of ten, where I summoned the courage to share my aspirations with my parents—to study overseas. Witness the seed of this dream take root within me as the flickering flame of possibility dances in my eyes. Years pass, and fate weaves its intricate tapestry, introducing me to a visa lottery program at the age of sixteen—a potential gateway to my envisioned future. The weight of financial constraints forces me to temporarily set aside my dreams, but destiny works in mysterious ways; a year later, the program resurfaces, reigniting the flickering flame within my heart.

## Divine Timing and Courageous Action

They say there is a time for every purpose under heaven, and that morning, as the visa lottery announcement echoes over the radio waves, a palpable energy fills the air. It feels different, as if the universe has conspired to align the stars in my favor. With unwavering determination, I muster the courage to approach my parents and request 800 naira, an amount that holds the key to my dreams. Despite their initial hesitation, my parents recognize the fire burning within me, embracing their son's fervor and agreeing to support my enrollment in the program. Little do they know that this humble step will change the course of our lives forever.

## The Journey Begins

Witness my joy and gratitude as I emerge as one of the chosen winners in the visa lottery. Feel the ground tremble beneath my feet as I step onto the soil of the United States of America, a land that holds promises as vast as the horizon. Yet I soon realize that the path to my aspirations is not as effortless as I had imagined. It is here that I discover the importance of shedding misconceptions and embracing the reality that true success demands unwavering determination and unrelenting effort. This newfound perspective becomes the catalyst for my growth and transformation.

## Unveiling the Path of Purpose

Imagine me entering college as a wide-eyed individual, caught up in the whirlwind of opinions about the "right" field of study for me to take on in the US. Amid the cacophony of voices, I feel lost, unsure of my true calling, but then, the Divine intervenes, disrupting my plans and compelling me to pause and reflect on my purpose. In a moment of revelation, I realize that my calling lies not in pharmacy, as I initially intended to pursue, but in a different discipline altogether. Memories resurface, the sparks of inspiration from my high school days, the desire to heal and bring hope to those plagued by illness. It is at that moment that I know my true calling is to become a physician.

## Lessons in Faith and Spiritual Growth

Step into the halls of medical school, where my acceptance marks the beginning of an arduous yet profoundly enlightening phase of my journey. Here, I am tested, time and again, by circumstances that drain my hope and challenge my faith. Yet, through these tribulations, I discover the immeasurable power of faith and the invaluable lessons hidden within the darkest moments. Guided by divine wisdom, I learn the art of spiritual warfare, the significance of walking hand in hand with the Almighty, and the ability to manifest change even in seemingly hopeless situations. These trials unveil the depths of my resilience and strengthen my connection with the Divine.

## A Call to Embrace Your Extraordinary Journey

As this first chapter draws to a close, I implore you to delve into your own journey. Within the depths of your being lies a potential beyond measure—a potential waiting to be unleashed. Embrace the whispers of your soul, the visions that surpass the ordinary, and the divine timing that orchestrates your path. With courage and unwavering determination, you can transcend limitations and manifest greatness in your life. Prepare to walk alongside me as we unravel the transformative lessons that await you in the chapters ahead. Let your journey of self-discovery and fulfillment begin.

## Actionable Steps

**Embrace Self-Reflection**: Take time to reflect on your own journey. Explore the whispers of your soul and identify the gentle nudges that ignite a belief in your extraordinary potential. Journal your thoughts, dreams, and aspirations, allowing yourself to envision a life that transcends limitations.

**Define Your Vision**: Nurture a powerful vision that redefines your life's trajectory. Dig deep within yourself and identify what truly ignites your passion and purpose. Write down your vision in vivid detail, capturing the essence of what you want to achieve and the impact you desire to make.

**Overcome Limiting Beliefs**: Shed misconceptions and self-imposed limitations that hinder your progress. Challenge negative thoughts and replace them with empowering affirmations. Recognize that true success demands unwavering determination and the willingness to embrace the journey, even when faced with obstacles.

**Take Courageous Action:** Understand that divine timing often aligns with your readiness to take action. Summon your courage and seize opportunities that come your way. Whether it's reaching out to someone for support, pursuing educational or professional opportunities, or taking the first step toward your dreams, embrace the unknown with faith and determination.

**Cultivate Faith and Resilience:** Strengthen your faith by embracing the lessons hidden within challenges. Trust in a higher power and develop a spiritual connection that sustains you through difficult times. Practice gratitude and mindfulness to nurture resilience and maintain a positive mindset.

**Seek Alignment with Your Purpose**: Continuously reassess your journey and realign with your true calling. Pause and reflect on the path you are on, ensuring that it aligns with your deepest values and aspirations. Be open to redirection and embrace the possibility of pursuing a different path that resonates with your soul.

**Take Inspired Action**: Move beyond contemplation and actively pursue opportunities for growth and self-discovery. Engage in activities, courses, or experiences that nurture your passions and expand your knowledge. Commit to life-long learning and embrace every opportunity to enhance your skills and broaden your horizons.

**Surround Yourself with Supportive Relationships**: Seek out individuals who believe in your potential and support your aspirations. Surround yourself with a positive and empowering network that encourages your growth and uplifts your spirit. Engage in communities or support groups that share similar goals, where you can find guidance, inspiration, and accountability.

**Embrace the Journey**: Understand that your journey is a process of growth and self-evolution. Embrace the ups and downs, knowing that each experience contributes to your transformation. Celebrate your progress, no matter how small, and remain committed to the path of self-discovery and fulfillment.

**Practice Self-Care**: Prioritize your well-being throughout the journey. Take care of your physical, mental, and emotional health. Nourish your body with nutritious food, engage in regular exercise, and practice self-reflection and self-care activities that rejuvenate your spirit. Remember, self-care is essential for maintaining balance and sustaining your momentum.

By integrating these actionable steps into your life, you will embark on a journey of self-discovery, unleash your extraordinary potential, and manifest greatness in every aspect of your life. Embrace the adventure that awaits you, and let your journey toward fulfillment and self-realization begin.

_____

_____

_____

_____

_____

_____

_____

_____

_____

_____

_____

_____

_____

_____

# CHAPTER 2

# From Uncertainty to Certainty

*Embracing the Known and the Unknown*

In the depths of my soul-stirring journey, fueled by divine encounters, I now embarked on a profound exploration of the known and the unknown. These contrasting realms shape our lives, leaving an indelible mark on our faith. Guided by the unwavering presence of the Holy Spirit, let us unlock the invaluable lessons we can garner by traversing these realms and infuse them into our personal odysseys. Prepare to be enthralled by the extraordinary expedition that awaits you—an expedition of self-discovery, growth, and resolute transformation.

## Shifting Mindsets: Could Be and Should Be

Within the vast tapestry of our existence, we encounter two powerful mindsets that dramatically influence our perspectives and actions. The phrase "could be" depicts a realm of uncertainty, where possibilities are acknowledged, but doubts cast shadows upon their realization. This mindset is a breeding ground for stagnation, doubt, and an overwhelming feeling of entrapment, which hinders our personal growth. However, the "should be" mindset illuminates our path with decisiveness and optimism, underscoring the potential for things to manifest themselves in our world. It sets ablaze the fire of hope, fortitude, and unwavering faith, empowering us to fearlessly embrace life's challenges and seize its opportunities. These mindsets lay the very foundation of our approach to life, intricately shaping our destiny along the way.

## Transitioning from Uncertainty to Certainty

The transition from uncertainty to certainty holds the key to revitalize our lives when we are plagued by prolonged doubts and insecurities. As we venture into the intricate recesses of the Divine Mind, uncovering His profound plans for the knowns and unknowns of our existence, I implore you to embark on this transformative journey with a prayerful heart. Pause and reflect when a word resonates within you, for it is in those sacred moments that divine guidance unfolds in extraordinary ways. Brace yourself for the profound shift from uncertainty to unshakable certainty that lies ahead, rekindling the flickering embers of hope and promising an unwavering future.

## Constants and Variables: Navigating the Known and the Unknown

To fathom the essence of the known and the unknown, we must grasp their profound significance. The known represents God's Word, promises, commands, and the visions and dreams He has gracefully infused within our hearts. It stands as an unchanging constant, a guiding star that illuminates our path even in the darkest of nights. Picture Father Abraham, who boldly embraced the known through God's command to leave behind his familiar shores and kin. On the other hand, the unknown embodies variables—elements yet to be revealed, mysteries awaiting their grand unveiling. It is through an unwavering trust in God's promises that Abraham embarked on a remarkable expedition into the unknown, guided solely by the unbreakable chains of faith.

## Embracing the Journey into the Unknown

To traverse the uncharted territories and divine destinies that God has intricately woven for us, we must consciously and wholeheartedly choose to follow Him. By anchoring ourselves to His Word, surrendering to His will and allowing Him to lead us into the vast realm of the unknown, we display unwavering faith and obedience. In this act of surrender, we acknowledge that God holds the key to what lies ahead and that He will reveal it to us in His perfect timing. Embracing the unknown becomes an invitation to a purposeful and fulfilling life, where our divine destinies unfurl before us like blossoming petals kissed by the morning dew.

## Anchoring Faith in the Constant Nature of God

In the tapestry of life, where circumstances shift like sand dunes in the wind, God's Word stands as an unwavering constant, transcending the transient nature of earthly realms. For Abraham to obediently follow God's command, he had to anchor himself to the constant factor—the immutable nature of God's Word—and trust that the variables of the unknown would align with His faithful promises. Similarly, we must recognize that God is unchanging and faithful. Every good and perfect gift originates from Him, and His nature remains unwavering through the ebb and flow of time. By grounding our faith in His steadfast nature, we find the assurance and confidence to embrace His promises, knowing that He will unwaveringly fulfill them.

## Conclusion: Embracing Certainty through Trust

As we conclude this chapter, we stand on the precipice of a remarkable transformation. By embracing the known and the unknown, shifting our mindsets, and trusting in God's unwavering promises, we unlock the power to transition from a life cloaked in uncertainty to one anchored in unwavering certainty. Remember, the path to certainty is illuminated by blind obedience, unwavering trust, and an unyielding faith in God's promises. Embrace this transformative journey and prepare to witness the extraordinary fulfillment of your divine purpose and destiny. The certainty you long for, the certainty your soul craves, is within your grasp.

## Actionable Steps

**Paint Your Mindset:** Close your eyes and vividly visualize your current mindset, especially whether it leans toward the realm of "could be" or "should be." Observe how this mindset colors your thoughts, decisions, and actions.

**Conquer Limiting Beliefs:** Consciously uncover any limiting beliefs that are preventing you from making the transition from uncertainty to certainty. Replace them with vibrant, empowering beliefs that resonate with your faith and resolute conviction in God's promises.

**Cultivate Trust:** Tend to your sacred garden of trust in God, nurturing it with prayer, meditation, and other spiritual practices that deepen your connection with the Divine. Watch as unwavering faith blossoms, carrying you through even the most treacherous terrains.

**Embrace the Unknown:** Summon the audacity to step out of your familiar abode, embracing opportunities that lie within the realm of the unknown. Trust that God, the Ultimate Guide, will navigate you over uncharted waters, unveiling your purpose as you courageously embark on this transformative journey.

**Engrave God's Word**: Immerse yourself in the sacred script of God's Word. Engage in study, meditation, and reflection, for within those hallowed pages lie wisdom, guidance, and unwavering truths that anchor your soul.

**Surrender and Obey**: Surrender your will to the Divine Hand, relinquishing control to God's purposeful leading. Obey His commands and heed His gentle whisper, even when it leads you to uncharted territories. Trust that in His hands, the unknown becomes a canvas on which He paints the portrait of your purpose.

**Seek Companionship**: Surround yourself with a community of believers who illuminate your path and uplift your spirit. Seek mentors, join small groups, or partake in spiritual retreats where kindred souls join forces to support, guide, and hold you accountable on your transformative expedition.

**Embrace Patience**: Embrace the notion that the journey from uncertainty to unwavering certainty is a sacred pilgrimage that unfolds in divine timing. Practice patience with yourself and trust in God's orchestration, knowing that He is working behind the scenes to align the intricate pieces of your destiny.

**Chronicle the Odyssey**: Establish a sacred journal to document the profound experiences, revelations, and personal milestones along your transformative journey. These written testimonies will serve as a beacon of hope and a reminder of God's faithfulness in times of uncertainty.

**Celebrate Milestones:** Celebrate each milestone on your journey from uncertainty to certainty. Mark these significant moments with gratitude, reflection, and praise, acknowledging the divine intervention that has brought you closer to the unwavering assurance of God's promises.

Now, armed with these actionable steps, step forward with confidence, for the extraordinary fulfillment of your divine purpose and destiny awaits you. May your soul be anchored in unwavering certainty, guided by the radiant light of faith.

_____

_____

_____

_____

_____

_____

_____

_____

_____

_____

# CHAPTER 3

# Embrace the Journey

## Running with Hope in the Storms

## Introduction

In the previous chapters, we embarked on a journey of transformation, exploring the power of blind obedience, of unwavering trust in God's promises, and of the transition from uncertainty to unwavering certainty. Now, we enter a new phase, reminiscent of a high-speed race in which the air crackles with anticipation. Life presents its challenges, and during uncertain times, we must embrace the mindset of a fearless runner. Imagine yourself standing at the starting line, heart pounding, as the divine racecourse stretches out before you. With each step, the ground beneath your feet pulsates with purpose, for you are not alone in this race. The Almighty God stands as the coach, urging you forward as you navigate the twists and turns, surmounting obstacles with unwavering determination.

## Conquer the Storms and Chase Your Vision

### Life's Voyage: Soaring through the Skies

Imagine yourself embarking on an exhilarating adventure, soaring through the skies aboard a plane. The vast expanse of the atmosphere unfolds before you, filled with endless possibilities. But even amid the breathtaking beauty, there are moments of turbulence that jolt you from your seat. The plane rumbles, shaking your confidence as the pilot's voice crackles over the intercom, warning of impending changes in the weather. In these moments, the pilot's calm demeanor provides reassurance, but deep down, a twinge of unease lingers within you.

### Turbulence in Life: Weathering the Storms

Life, too, is filled with its share of turbulence. Just like our proverbial airline passengers, we often find ourselves facing unexpected challenges and storms that threaten to disrupt our journey. These turbulent times test our resolve, shake our confidence, and sometimes leave us feeling vulnerable and uncertain. It's in these moments that we must adopt the mindset of a determined runner, steadfastly focused on reaching the finish line of our goals and dreams, for within us resides an unyielding spirit, driven by the belief that we can overcome any adversity.

### Finding Comfort in the Pilot: God, the Almighty Guide

During those turbulent moments in life, it's important to find solace in the knowledge that the pilot of your life's plane is none other than the Almighty God. Imagine for a moment the Creator of the universe taking the helm, guiding your journey with unwavering wisdom and strength. With God as your pilot, you can be confident that He will steer you through the storms and lead you to safe havens. Trust in His guidance, and let His presence bring you comfort and assurance during the most challenging times.

## Embracing Hope and Overcoming Doubt

### The Runner's Mindset: Perseverance in the Face of Turbulence

As a runner on the track of life, you must develop a resilient mindset that propels you forward, even when you're faced with turbulence. Turbulent times may leave you feeling weary, tempted to give up, or unsure of your path. You may encounter unexpected opposition from people around you, including those you least expect. Doubt may creep in, prompting you to question your abilities and wonder if you're alone on your journey. Remember, you are not alone. Embrace the truth that you are the embodiment of hope, a testament to your strength in overcoming past storms.

*Igniting the Flame of Hope: Declare Your Power*

Imagine a surge of life and strength coursing through every fiber of your being as you boldly declare, "I am the embodiment of hope!" Visualize this flame of hope burning brightly within you, casting out fear and adversity. In moments of doubt and uncertainty, remind yourself of this truth. Believe in your capacity to conquer any obstacle and overcome any setback. Hope is a force that transcends fear, adversity, and cynicism. As you fight to keep that flame of hope alive, remember that the storms of life seek to halt your progress, but armed with the power of hope, press on. Keep running with your vision until it becomes a glorious reality.

## Running with the Vision: A Journey of Timing and Trust

*The Essence of Running with the Vision*

"Running with the vision" means embracing your journey from the known to the unknown. It requires a delicate balance between action and patience, between striving and surrendering. Running ahead of the vision, like Moses did, can have grave consequences. Moses, in his eagerness to fulfill his destiny, acted prematurely, altering the course of his journey and delaying the realization of his vision. Learn from this cautionary tale and understand that the timing of your vision is essential.

### Divine Timing: Trusting the Unseen Path

In life's journey, God's timing is impeccable. He orchestrates events and aligns circumstances in ways that may seem mysterious to us. Embrace the unknown, for it is within this realm that your vision will unfold. Trust in the divine timing of your dreams and desires. Just as Moses faced challenges when he ran ahead of his vision, recognize that impatience can hinder the manifestation of your purpose. Surrender the need to control every detail and instead embrace the unseen path that God is laying before you.

## Obedience and the Power of Alignment

### The Voice of God: Directing Your Path

What God says about you holds immeasurable power. Amid the multitude of voices in the world, it is His voice that holds the key to unlocking your true potential. Take a moment to reflect on what God is saying to you right now. Consider the visions, dreams, and ideas He has placed within your heart. These whispers of purpose carry the potential to transform your life and the lives of those around you.

### Embracing Obedience: Aligning with Divine Guidance

When God places His divine finger on your purpose, it's time to act. Embrace obedience as the gateway to running with the vision. Like Abraham, who departed as the Lord had spoken to him, take a step in faith and align your actions with God's guidance (Genesis 12:4). Obedience serves as the cornerstone of your journey. It sets in motion a series of events that align with God's plan, transforming you into a vessel through which His purpose will manifest.

### The Power of Alignment: Becoming a Vessel of Divine Purpose

Complete obedience unlocks the extraordinary in your life. By aligning your actions with God's commands, you become a vessel for His divine purpose. Every intricate detail of your life holds significance to Him. Your relationships, education, career, family, and even personal struggles become part of God's grand tapestry. You are chosen to shine forth His praises and illuminate the world with the brilliance of His light.

## Holding On to the Promise

### The Unwavering Word: Counting on God's Promises

In the face of uncertainty, hold fast to the unwavering Word of God. While you may not have all the details of how His promises will come to pass, trust in His faithfulness. Storms may rage and challenges may arise, but the reassurance of God's Word will sustain you. Remember that He has exalted His Word above His very name. It is a solid foundation on which you can stand, unwavering and unshaken.

### *The Journey Continues: A Call to Openness and Exploration*

As we journey forward, this book takes a dramatic turn, unveiling profound revelations and insights prepared specifically for this moment. Regardless of your beliefs, approach the following chapters with an open mind and a receptive heart. Allow the wisdom shared here to resonate within you, leading you to new perspectives and possibilities. May you be blessed as you continue reading, discovering the transformative power that awaits you.

## Actionable Steps

**Reflect on Life's Voyage**: Take a moment to visualize your life's journey as a thrilling adventure. Embrace the highs and lows, and recognize that turbulence is a natural part of the experience.

**Embrace Resilience**: Cultivate a runner's mindset by developing perseverance in the face of adversity. Remind yourself that challenges are opportunities for growth and learning.

**Seek Comfort in God's Guidance**: Find solace in the unwavering belief that God, the ultimate guiding force, is present in your life's journey. Trust in His divine guidance as you navigate through the storms, knowing that He is leading you toward your desired destination. Embrace the comforting presence of God, recognizing that His wisdom and love will guide you through every challenge and uncertainty.

**Ignite the Flame of Hope:** Declare affirmations that reinforce your belief in your abilities and in the power of hope. Visualize a bright flame of hope burning within you, dispelling doubt and fear.

**Conquer Self-Doubt:** When doubt creeps in, remind yourself of past triumphs and the strength you have shown in overcoming challenges. Surround yourself with positive influences and support systems that encourage your belief in yourself.

**Embrace Divine Timing:** Recognize that everything happens in its own time. Instead of rushing ahead, practice patience and trust the timing of your vision. Focus on making the most of the present moment while remaining open to the unfolding of your path.

**Listen to the Voice of Guidance:** Pay attention to the inner nudges and external signs that may guide you toward your purpose. Take time to connect with your intuition and discern what feels aligned with your vision and values.

**Act in Obedience:** When you receive clear guidance or a sense of divine direction, take action. Trust in the power of your obedience to align your actions with the unfolding of your purpose.

**Seek Alignment in All Areas of Life:** Reflect on the different aspects of your life, such as relationships, education, career, and personal growth. Evaluate whether these areas align with your vision and values. Make adjustments as necessary to ensure congruence between your actions and your purpose.

**Anchor Yourself in God's Promises**: Continually remind yourself of the unwavering nature of God's promises. Draw strength from the reassurance that, despite challenges, His Word remains steadfast and will come to fruition.

**Stay Open and Curious**: Approach each new experience with openness and a willingness to explore. Remain receptive to the insights and revelations that come your way, even if they challenge your existing beliefs.

**Take Action**: Apply the wisdom gained from this book and the insights you've received to your everyday life. Implement actionable steps, make necessary changes, and continue pursuing your vision with renewed determination.

Remember, the ultimate goal is to run with your vision, conquer the storms, and achieve fulfillment in alignment with your purpose. Stay committed to the journey, and trust that as you take each step, you are moving closer to the manifestation of your dreams.

_____

_____

_____

_____

_____

# CHAPTER 4

# When Dreams Clash with Reality

## A Trying-of-Faith Moment

### A Vision of Hope

As I embarked on my journey through the maze of medical training, a glimmer of hope shone upon my path. The Lord graced me with a vision, a divine revelation that whispered of a positive outcome to the pursuit I held dear. It was a beacon of light after a prior disappointment, filling my heart with renewed anticipation. Believing every word He had spoken, I forged ahead with unwavering faith. I could almost taste the victory that lay ahead.

### Tears on the Floor: Embracing Resilience in the Face of Adversity

Life has a way of testing our resolve, of shaking the very foundation on which our dreams rest. When my long-awaited outcome finally unfolded, it struck me like a thunderbolt.

Undesirable. Unfathomable. My world crumbled around me, and I found myself collapsed on the floor of my Atlanta apartment, tears streaming down my face. The weight of devastation bore heavily upon my shoulders, and I cried out to the heavens, seeking answers.

## Wrestling with the Divine

In the midst of my anguish, I pleaded with the Almighty, questioning His plans. "God, this is not what you told me!" I cried, my voice echoing through the room. Confusion and doubt gnawed at my soul as I grappled with the misalignment between His promise and my reality. I had prayed. I had fasted. Where had I gone wrong? These questions hung in the air, unanswered.

## The Solace of Love

In the depths of my despair, my then fiancée stood by my side, offering solace and compassion. She extended her gentle touch and tender words, attempting to ease the torment that gripped my heart. I wept, releasing my pain like a helpless child. The blow to my faith reverberated within me, threatening to extinguish the flickering flame of hope.

## Embracing the Assurance

In the midst of the darkness that enveloped my soul, a faint whisper emerged—a voice of assurance cutting through the turmoil. The voice of God reminded me of His unwavering presence and unyielding love. "When I fall, I shall rise; when I sit in darkness, the Lord shall be a light unto me." – Micah 7:8. It was a lifeline of hope, a reminder that even in the face of shattered expectations, God's light could guide me out of the darkest depths.

## Navigating the Chasm: Doubt Defeated, Faith Rekindled in Unwavering Promises

In the footsteps of Abraham, I found myself questioning the promises that had stirred my soul. The chasm between God's assurances and the stark reality before me seemed insurmountable. Doubt and uncertainty gnawed at my faith, threatening to dismantle the foundation on which my dreams were built, but I soon discovered that the impossibility we perceive is but an ephemeral illusion, a mere whisper in the face of God's unwavering promises.

## Resilience in the Face of Adversity: Fueling Hope Amid Shattered Dreams

Life's journey often takes us through the shadowed valleys, where our dreams clash with the harsh realities of the world. Yet, within these shadows, hope flickers, refusing to be extinguished. It is here, in the face of shattered expectations, that we find the strength to rise once more and press on.

## Lessons in Perseverance

Like a diamond forged under intense pressure, we are called to embrace our trials as opportunities for growth. The trying-of-faith moments become catalysts for transformation, shaping us into individuals with greater resilience and wisdom. We discover that God's plans may not always align with our desires, but His purpose remains unwavering, polishing us into the best version of ourselves.

## Rediscovering Faith's Resilience

In the aftermath of disappointment, we are challenged to rediscover the resilience of our faith. It is not a faith that wavers with every setback but one that finds strength in surrender and trust. Through tears and questions, we learn to surrender our plans and seek solace in His unwavering love.

## The Light in the Darkness

As we navigate the darkness, we must remember that even in the bleakest moments, God's light still shines. His presence becomes the guiding star that illuminates our path, leading us through our trials and toward a greater purpose. In the surrender of our shattered expectations, we find the courage to embrace the unknown and trust in His divine plan.

## A Symphony of Hope

The storms of life may temporarily dampen our spirits, but they cannot extinguish the flame of hope within us.

Like a symphony that crescendos after a momentary pause, our journey continues. We pick ourselves up, dust off the remnants of disappointment, and with renewed faith, we march forward, trusting that every step brings us closer to the fulfillment of our purpose.

## The Unveiling of Destiny

Beyond the mountain of uncertainty and the illusion of impossibility lies the unveiling of our destiny. In the face of adversity, we are molded, refined, and transformed into the glorious sons and daughters God destined us to be. So let us defy the storms, embrace the trials, and trust that even in the darkest moments, our destiny awaits, radiant and full of promise.

## Embrace Uncertainty:
### Unlock Boundless Power on an Extraordinary Journey of Self-Discovery

Prepare yourself for an extraordinary expedition into the realm of uncertainty, where faith and destiny intertwine in a dance of breathtaking magnitude. Brace yourself for the unveiling of your true potential as you navigate the uncharted territories, guided by the unbreakable bond between your faith and your purpose. Embrace uncertainty, for within its grasp lies the catalyst for your transformation, the key to unlocking the boundless power that resides within your soul.

# Actionable Steps

**Reflect on the Vision of Hope:** Take time to recall and meditate on the initial vision or divine revelation that filled your heart with hope and anticipation. Revisit the details and the positive outcome it whispered about, allowing it to renew your faith and determination.

**Embrace Resilience:** Recognize that life has a way of testing our resolve and that adversity is a natural part of the journey. When faced with undesirable and unfathomable outcomes, acknowledge the pain and allow yourself to grieve. Then, embrace resilience by acknowledging your emotions, seeking support, and finding healthy ways to process your experience.

**Seek Answers in Faith:** In moments of anguish and doubt, engage in a dialogue with the Divine. Pour out your heart, questioning the misalignment between God's promise and your reality. Allow yourself to wrestle with these questions, seeking understanding and His guidance through prayer and introspection.

**Find Solace in Relationships:** Surround yourself with loved ones who can offer solace and compassion during your moments of despair. Lean on their support, allowing their gentle touch and tender words to ease the torment that grips your heart. Share your pain and allow yourself to be vulnerable, finding comfort in the presence of those who care about you.

**Hold On To the Assurance**: In the midst of darkness, listen for the faint whisper of assurance that cuts through the turmoil. Remind yourself of God's unwavering presence and unyielding love. Reflect on scriptural verses or passages that offer hope and reassurance, such as Micah 7:8, and let these words become a lifeline of hope that guides you out of the darkest depths.

**Overcome Doubt with Faith**: Just as Abraham questioned the promises that stirred his soul, recognize that doubt and uncertainty may gnaw at your faith. However, discover that the chasm between God's assurances and your reality is not insurmountable. Challenge the ephemeral illusion of impossibility and reaffirm your faith in God's unwavering promises, knowing that He can bring forth the extraordinary from the ordinary.

**Cultivate Resilience in Shattered Dreams**: Embrace the strength to rise once more and press on in the face of shattered expectations. Acknowledge the clash between your dreams and the harsh realities of the world, but let hope flicker within you, refusing to be extinguished. Draw on your inner resilience, finding the courage and determination to navigate the challenges and continue moving forward.

**Learn from Perseverance**: Embrace the trials and trying-of-faith moments as catalysts for growth. Recognize that these experiences shape you into an individual with greater resilience and wisdom. Allow yourself to be polished, like a diamond forged under intense pressure, trusting that God's purpose remains steadfast even when His plans do not align with your desires.

**Rediscover Faith's Resilience**: Challenge yourself to rediscover the resilience of your faith. Move beyond setbacks and disappointments, cultivating a faith that is unwavering in the face of adversity. Surrender your plans and desires, seeking solace and strength in God's unwavering love. Let go of wavering faith and embrace a steadfast trust in His divine guidance.

**Embrace the Light in the Darkness**: Remember that even in the bleakest moments, God's light still shines. Allow His presence to become the guiding star that illuminates your path. Embrace the surrender of your shattered expectations, finding the courage to step into the unknown and trust in His greater purpose. Let His light lead you through your trials toward a fulfilling and meaningful destination.

**Sustain Hope as a Symphony**: Recognize that the storms of life may temporarily dampen your spirits, but they cannot extinguish the flame of hope within you. Embrace the metaphorical symphony that continues to crescendo after momentary pauses. Pick yourself up, dust off the remnants of disappointment, and march forward with renewed faith, knowing that every step brings you closer to the fulfillment of your purpose.

**Unveil Your Destiny**: Journey beyond the mountain of uncertainty and the illusion of impossibility. Embrace the unveiling of your destiny, recognizing that adversity molds, refines, and transforms you into the glorious individual that God destined you to be. Defy the storms, embrace the trials, and trust that even in the darkest moments, your destiny awaits you, radiant and full of promise.

With these actionable steps, you are equipped to embrace uncertainty, test your faith, and emerge victorious in the face of the unknown. Embrace the journey that lies ahead, for it is through the trials and triumphs that the true essence of your faith is revealed.

_____

_____

_____

_____

_____

_____

_____

_____

_____

_____

_____

_____

_____

_____

_____

_____

_____

_____

_____

_____

_____

_____

_____

_____

_____

_____

_____

_____

_____

# CHAPTER 5

# Alignment with God

## God's Grand Design: Embracing the Potter's Wheel

Step into the world of the prophet Jeremiah as we unravel the captivating concept of alignment with God. Imagine standing in a bustling potter's shop, where clay takes shape under the skilled hands of a potter. This simple scene holds a profound lesson about our alignment with the Creator.

In this chapter, we will explore how God's grand design for our lives calls us to be like Him and to conform to His will. However, the distractions and influences of the world often pull us away from this divine alignment. Just as the potter molds and remolds the clay until it conforms to his desired shape, God molds and remolds us to align with His will.

## The Ripple Effects of Misalignment: Lessons from the Children of Israel

The pages of history unfold to reveal powerful stories of misalignment with God's will and its far-reaching consequences. Let's journey back to ancient times and witness the plight of the children of Israel. Their failure to honor the Sabbath, a commandment from God Himself, led to their enslavement by their enemies for a staggering seventy years. Intriguingly, their misalignment resulted in their displacement from the promised land (2 Chronicles 36:20–21), a place overflowing with blessings and freedom. Therefore, it becomes evident that when we walk contrary to God's will, we jeopardize the very promises and destinies He has in store for us.

## Breaking and Remaking: The Divine Process of Transformation

Prepare to be captivated by the dramatic tale of King Nebuchadnezzar and his encounter with the breaking power of God. Filled with pride, Nebuchadnezzar attributed his achievements solely to himself, failing to acknowledge God's role in his success. As a consequence, he experienced a staggering downfall that left him stripped of his sanity, reduced to living like a beast for seven long years.

This divine breaking process was not meant to destroy Nebuchadnezzar, but rather to rebuild him into a humbler, more obedient servant of God. It serves as a powerful reminder that the challenges we sometimes face are part of God's divine orchestration to realign us with His will. Before Nebuchadnezzar's breaking, God sent him a dream as a warning, providing an opportunity for repentance and alignment. Yet pride clouded his judgment, leading to his ultimate fate.

## Acknowledging God's Supremacy: Shattering the Shackles of Pride

Pride, the formidable foe of our true alignment with God, takes center stage in this section. Its subtle manifestations can hinder our journey of alignment, leading us down a treacherous path. Whether it's looking down on others, boasting of our accomplishments, or failing to attribute our success to God, pride robs us of the very intimacy and blessings that alignment offers.

But fear not! We have the power to shatter the shackles of pride by acknowledging God's supremacy in our lives. Reflect on the cautionary tale of Nebuchadnezzar and embrace the life-transforming virtue of humility, for it is the humble who receive God's grace while the proud find themselves resisted by the divine hand.

## Embracing the Breaking Process: Unveiling Beauty from the Ashes

In a world where brokenness is often seen as a mark of failure, we unveil a revolutionary perspective: God's breaking is not intended to crush us indefinitely but to shape us into something more beautiful and more aligned with His will. The trials, setbacks, and moments of breaking in our lives hold the potential for incredible transformation and growth.

Instead of resenting these moments, let us embrace them with open hearts and minds. As we willingly align with God's will, we invite His grace, guidance, and blessings into our lives. The breaking process becomes an opportunity for us to actively participate in our own transformation instead of passively awaiting divine intervention.

## The Journey of Alignment: A Divine Communion

Now, we embark on an awe-inspiring journey—a journey of alignment with the Creator of the universe. As we surrender our will to His, we experience a deeper communion with Him and uncover the true fulfillment and purpose He has designed for our lives. Together, let us willingly conform to His perfect plan, allowing Him to shape us according to His divine blueprint.

## Conclusion

Prepare yourself for a transformational expedition that will captivate your heart, challenge your perspectives, and leave you yearning for a more profound alignment with God. Join me as we delve into the profound mysteries of alignment and unlock the transformative power that lies within.

## Actionable Steps

**Seek Daily Communion**: Seek daily communion with God through prayer and meditation. Set aside dedicated time to connect with the divine presence and listen for His guidance. Create a sacred space where you can retreat and foster a deeper relationship with Him.

**Reflect**: Engage in self-reflection and introspection to identify areas of misalignment in your life. Examine your thoughts, actions, and attitudes, and honestly assess whether they align with God's principles and will. Be open to receiving correction and guidance from the Holy Spirit.

**Study the Word of God**: Delve into the Scriptures to gain wisdom, understanding, and insights into God's character and His desired path for your life. Let His Word serve as a guiding light, illuminating the way toward alignment with Him.

**Cultivate a Posture of Surrender and Obedience**: Practice yielding your will to God's will, even when it goes against your own desires or plans. Develop a trust in His wisdom and sovereignty, knowing that His plans are greater than your own.

**Seek Community**: Surround yourself with a community of believers who are also seeking alignment with God. Engage in fellowship, share insights, and support one another in your individual journeys toward alignment. Seek mentors or spiritual leaders who can provide guidance and accountability.

**Welcome the Change**: Embrace the breaking process as an opportunity for growth and transformation. When faced with challenges or moments of breaking, surrender to God's refining work in your life. Trust that He is molding you into a vessel aligned with His purposes, even in the midst of discomfort.

**Practice Humility in All Areas of Your Life**: Cultivate a heart of gratitude, recognizing that every good thing comes from God. Acknowledge His supremacy and give Him credit for your achievements and blessings. Seek opportunities to serve others, humbly recognizing the value and worth of every individual.

**Re-Evaluate**: Regularly evaluate and realign your priorities and goals with God's will. Continuously assess whether your pursuits and ambitions are in harmony with His purposes.

Be willing to let go of anything that hinders your alignment and embrace new directions that align with His calling.

By implementing these actionable steps, you will embark on a transformative journey of alignment with God. Allow His hands to mold and shape you, revealing the beauty and purpose that lie within. Embrace the divine communion that awaits you as you align your heart, mind, and actions with the Creator of all things.

_____

_____

_____

_____

_____

_____

_____

_____

_____

_____

_____

_____

# CHAPTER 6

# Unleashing the Power Within
## A Journey to Glorious Fulfillment

## The Race of Destiny: Embracing the Divine Purpose

In the pursuit of our dreams, we discover that our lives are not simply a meandering journey but an exhilarating race toward a divine purpose. It is a race filled with twists and turns, where some falter and others endure brutal attacks along the way. In the grand scheme of things, it is the grace of God that ultimately determines who emerges victorious at the finish line.

From the very moment a child takes their first breath, the race to fulfill God's purpose commences. But let us not forget, there are races, and then there are races! The remarkable races in life, when triumphantly completed, become gateways to promotion and fulfillment beyond measure. One such extraordinary race etched in history was Jesus's epic journey from Gabbatha to Golgotha. It was a race that pushed the boundaries of His endurance and tested His unwavering determination to finish victoriously. The anticipation of the "joy that was set before Him" propelled Him to endure the weight of the cross and despise the shame that accompanied it.

Jesus possessed an unwavering certainty that, beyond the finish line, glory awaited Him. He foresaw the moment when His name would ascend to the highest authority, causing every knee in heaven, on earth, and under the earth to bow in reverence. Every tongue, irrespective of agreement or disagreement, would be compelled to confess that He is Lord. Jesus caught a glimpse of the magnificence that would follow His race to Golgotha, the place of glorification, and He was prepared to endure the pain because He understood its temporary nature. It shall pass, just as your pain and sorrow will soon dissipate.

## Embracing the Glory: A Source of Unyielding Resolve

Let the glory that awaits you become an unshakable impetus that propels you forward on your journey. Even in moments when you feel like surrendering, envision the splendor, joy, and new life that lie ahead. Embrace this vision wholeheartedly, and even in the midst of overwhelming challenges, a deep well of joy will spring forth from within you.

In this race of destiny, endurance becomes your ally, and the weight of the cross you bear becomes a symbol of your unwavering commitment. Disregard the voices of ridicule and doubt that seek to undermine your progress. Remember, you have the promise of a future that transcends your wildest imagination, for God Himself runs this race with you. His grace is the invisible force propelling you forward, ensuring that you reach the finish line in resplendent glory.

## The Power to Overcome: Igniting Resilience

Embrace the pain that accompanies this race of destiny. Embrace it, knowing that it is in the crucible of challenges that your true strength is forged. Bear the weight of your cross with unwavering courage, for in doing so, you demonstrate your commitment to the higher purpose that beckons you. Ignore the ridicule that seeks to deter you, for you are not alone on this journey. The promise of a glorious future with God is your constant companion, providing unwavering support and guidance.

Amid trials and tribulations, I implore you to press on with tenacity and unwavering resolve. Your pain is but a temporary affliction compared to the eternal victory that awaits you. With every step, you draw closer to the finish line, where your faithfulness and endurance will be crowned with divine glory. The world may tempt you to give up, but I urge you to remain steadfast and resolute.

### The Elevation of Triumph: A Glorious Arrival

At the culmination of this remarkable race, envision the moment of triumph when you cross the finish line in resplendent victory. Picture the radiant glow of fulfillment and the overwhelming joy that envelops your being. It is here that you will witness the transformative power of God's grace, elevating you to unimaginable heights.

*Conclusion:*

In this journey of self-discovery and purpose, may you find the strength to endure, the courage to bear your cross, and the resilience to overcome every obstacle. I pray that the grace of God guides your every step and that you emerge from this race gloriously, basking in the radiant light of your extraordinary destiny.

## Actionable Steps

**Define Your Divine Purpose**: Take time to reflect and seek God's guidance in discovering your unique purpose in life. Engage in self-reflection and prayer, and seek wise counsel to gain clarity on the path you are called to walk.

**Set Clear Goals**: Break down your divine purpose into actionable and measurable goals. Write them down and create a plan to achieve them. Make sure your goals align with God's principles and contribute to the fulfillment of your purpose.

**Develop Unwavering Resolve:** Cultivate a mindset of determination and resilience. Embrace the challenges that come your way as opportunities for growth and character development. When you are faced with obstacles, choose to persevere, relying on God's strength and grace to carry you through.

**Visualize the Glory that Awaits You:** Create a vivid vision of the glorious outcome that awaits you at the finish line of your race. Visualize the joy, fulfillment, and impact that will come from fulfilling your divine purpose. Use this vision as motivation during difficult times and as a reminder of the rewards that await your perseverance.

**Seek Divine Guidance and Strength:** Regularly seek God's guidance through prayer and meditation. Develop a habit of listening to the Holy Spirit's promptings and aligning your actions with His leading. Draw strength from your relationship with God, knowing that He is running the race with you, providing the grace and support you need.

**Surround Yourself with a Supportive Community:** Seek out like-minded individuals who are also pursuing their divine purposes. Engage in fellowship, share experiences, and encourage one another along the journey. Consider joining a small group or community that can provide accountability and support.

**Embrace Challenges as Opportunities for Growth:** Shift your perspective on challenges and setbacks. Instead of viewing them as obstacles, see them as stepping stones toward your ultimate victory. Learn from your failures, adjust your approach, and keep moving forward with renewed determination.

**Stay Focused and Eliminate Distractions**: Identify and eliminate distractions that hinder your progress. Evaluate how you spend your time, energy, and resources, ensuring that they align with your divine purpose. Prioritize activities and relationships that contribute to your growth and fulfillment.

**Celebrate Milestones along the Way**: Acknowledge and celebrate the milestones and accomplishments you've achieved on your journey. Take time to reflect on how far you've come and express gratitude for God's faithfulness. Celebrate these moments as markers of progress and encouragement to keep pressing forward.

**Trust in God's Timing**: Remember that God's timing is perfect. Be patient and trust that He will fulfill His promises in His perfect timing. Resist the urge to compare your progress or success with others, and instead focus on faithfully running your own race.

By taking these actionable steps, you embark on a transformative journey to unleash the power within and pursue a glorious fulfillment of your divine purpose. Embrace the race with determination, resilience, and unwavering trust in God's guidance. Through His grace, you will cross the finish line victoriously and experience the transformative elevation of triumph in fulfilling your extraordinary destiny.

# CHAPTER 7

# Unleashing the Power Within

## Conquering Spiritual Antagonism

### Unveiling the Antagonists: Unmasking the Shadows

When our souls ignite with an unwavering determination to unearth our purpose, manifest our God-given dreams, and unlock the full extent of our potential, we embark on a voyage fraught with obstacles, temptations, trials, and even failures. These adversaries often trace their origins to an unseen realm of spiritual antagonism, yet, alas, many among us remain oblivious to the fact that we are caught in the clutches of such spiritual warfare. Instead, we perceive our problems as mere chance occurrences in the natural world.

But lo and behold, at the hallowed feet of the Lord, I have continued to glean a profound revelation—a revelation that pierces the veil between the natural and the spiritual. The truth unfurls before me like a majestic tapestry: the physical realm, with all its intricacies, dances to the symphony of the spirit realm.

"For we do not wrestle [war] against flesh and blood [the natural realm], but against [spirits of opposition, such as] principalities, against powers, against the rulers of the darkness of this age, against spiritual hosts of wickedness in the heavenly places" (Ephesians 6:12).

Until we fully embrace the existence of these spiritual antagonists, ceaselessly toiling to sow discord within the souls of living beings, even those who profess their faith in Christ, the cycle of antagonism shall persist. You may ask, "Why would I be subjected to such hostility? Have I offended anyone?" The answer, my friend, is as simple as it is profound. The audacity to embark on a journey to fulfill our purpose, to actualize our dreams, to maximize our potential, and to stand unwavering upon the bedrock of God's promises, it is an open invitation to be assaulted by the forces of darkness. In due course, you may find yourself ensnared in spiritual warfare you never could have anticipated. I myself stand as a living testament to this reality.

As I laid bare in the depths of Chapter 4, the crucible of my medical training subjected me to excruciating trials, leaving me shrouded in uncertainty about the path ahead. A recurring motif threaded through these painful ordeals: the sting of disappointment at the precipice of triumph. In the realm of the natural, I exerted every ounce of my being, employing every strategy within my grasp toward achieving success, only to watch my efforts falter. It was in those trying moments that I discerned a pattern emerging—a pattern rooted not in the physical, but in the spiritual. The forces of darkness, the devil and his agents, orchestrated a symphony of manipulation, intertwining the fibers of the natural and the spiritual to impede my success in the tangible world. Yet I lift my voice in exaltation to the Almighty God, the Great Deliverer, for He answered my plea. He became my refuge, my strength, an ever-present help in times of trouble (Psalm 46:1).

## Engaging in Spiritual Warfare: The Power of Prayer and Fasting

Caught in unwarranted spiritual warfare, I declared a seven-day fast, abstaining from food and water, to wage war against the kingdom of darkness. As I fervently pursued my success, I immersed myself in prayer. Prayer became my weapon, and as I prayed, I worked harder. It was a matter of life and death to seize what rightfully belonged to me.

Throughout my entire life, I have had to overcome the powers that attempted to hinder my progress. Though I did not know the exact source or reason for the antagonism, it did not deter me. My focus remained fixed on attaining victory through the power found in the name and blood of Jesus Christ. All that mattered was that Jesus Christ had been given a name above all names, and at the mention of

His name, every knee must bow—including those of the antagonists who were fighting against me.

Empowered by the Holy Spirit's righteous indignation, I persisted in prayer, refusing to leave the presence of God until I obtained my breakthrough. As the days of my fasting and prayer progressed, I witnessed a shifting of tides in the spiritual realm. My spiritual eyes were opened and able to discern the necessary adjustments and actions I needed to take to break through the barriers that had been set before me. God began illuminating my spiritual understanding, signaling that my breakthrough was drawing near.

On the seventh day of my fast, a profound dream unraveled before me. Its interpretation revealed that the battle was far from over. Realizing this, I resolved to undertake another seven-day fast while simultaneously intensifying my efforts toward achieving success. I was determined to prevail and willing to give it everything it would take.

During the midst of my second fast, on that momentous day of April 14, 2011, the Lord bestowed upon me my long-awaited breakthrough. He opened my eyes and granted me a revelation that forever transformed my life.

## The Revealing Dream: Seizing Victory

In the divine revelation, I found myself seated in the front row of an immense gathering, where thousands had assembled to celebrate my accomplishments. Waitstaff began serving food to all the attendees, but to my astonishment,

I realized that everyone in my row had been served except for me. Bewilderment engulfed me. If I was the one being celebrated, why was I being deprived of food?

Enraptured by the Spirit of God's fervor, a righteous anger ignited within me. With boldness drawn from the Lord, I made my way to the back of the hall, where the food was being prepared and distributed. What awaited me there was truly perplexing. I encountered a towering man, weighing possibly three to four hundred pounds, who was in charge of distributing the food. Filled with righteous indignation, I confronted him directly. "I am the one being celebrated, so why am I being denied food?" Compelled by the divine authority in my voice, he had no choice but to comply with my request.

He then proposed that I assist him in serving my own portion of food. Pointing to a colossal flask, he instructed me to retrieve my sustenance. As I opened the flask, I discovered that the food within it was frozen solid. Determined, I had to excavate the frozen sustenance and transfer it into a larger bowl, then allow the hefty man to warm it up for me. The sheer act of serving the food brought me immense joy, for I realized that my portion far exceeded that of those sitting in my row. The magnitude of my portion made me feel like the true celebrant.

However, as the man poured the food into a pot, he exclaimed that it was an excessive amount. He questioned whether he should pour all the food into the pot. In response, my elation overflowed, and with unwavering certainty, I declared, "Pour it all in. Pour everything!" The delight, elation, and overwhelming joy that engulfed me were unparalleled. Then, I awakened to the glorious reality of my victory. I spent the remaining days of my fast in unending thanksgiving, knowing full well that the battle had been won. To the eternal glory of the living God, just one month after this revelation, I triumphantly achieved what had eluded me for far too long.

## The Power of Spiritual Perception: Unlocking the Supernatural

Through these experiences and many others, I have gleaned invaluable insights, including an understanding that the physical realm is heavily influenced by the spiritual realm. I exerted my utmost efforts from a human standpoint, yet breakthroughs eluded me until I adopted a spiritual perspective to address my predicament. It was within the sacred realm of prayer that I found my solace and received divine intervention.

When we enter the secret place of the Most High, which is the abode of prayer and intimacy with God, we position ourselves under the protective shadow of the Almighty (Psalm 91:1). In this sacred abode, no power can withstand us. Shielded by His presence, darkness fades away, unable to comprehend the radiance of God. When we position ourselves in the very presence of God, every evil force contributing to our predicament must bow in submission.

"God also has highly exalted Him [Jesus Christ] and given Him the name which is above every name, that at the name of Jesus every knee should bow" (Philippians 2:9–10 NKJV). The mere presence of God compels every knee to bow! Without the presence of God upon me, the colossal man of darkness, presented in my dreams as the hefty server, would never have acquiesced to my directives. Without the presence of God, I would have remained oblivious to the back room, where decisions in the spiritual realm profoundly affected my life and my physical reality.

The presence of God propelled me into the spiritual realm, enabling me to witness these machinations at play. Moreover, His presence empowered me to reclaim what was rightfully mine, held captive under the pretense of being frozen. The frozen food, seemingly insignificant, masked the kingdom of darkness's attempt to impede my success in a particular area of my life. But I had sought solace within the place of prayer, pleading for God's intervention.

Eyes that merely look are commonplace, but eyes that truly see are rare gems. God graces us with the gift of spiritual sight, but we must thirst for it. We must beseech Him to open the eyes of our spirit, enabling us to perceive what the ordinary eye cannot. Our ears, too, require His touch to hear what the ordinary ear cannot.

## A Call to Arms: The Unveiling of Truth

Dear reader, as you embark upon your own odyssey to fulfill your purpose, to manifest your dreams, and to unlock the vast depths of your potential, I implore you to heed the revelations unveiled within these sacred pages. Arm yourself with the knowledge that you are not merely a casualty of circumstance, but a spiritual warrior. Open your eyes to the antagonists that seek to hinder your progress and lay waste to your destiny.

Embrace the power of prayer, allowing it to ignite within you an unquenchable flame of perseverance. Let the truth of God's Word be your guiding light, illuminating the path of victory that awaits you. With each step, with each breath, march forward with unwavering determination, for your purpose beckons, your destiny yearns to be realized.

In the realm of spiritual warfare, the battles may be arduous, the adversaries fierce, but take solace, dear reader, for the victory has already been won. In the triumphant name of Jesus Christ, we stand united, defying the forces of darkness and embracing the truth that we are more than conquerors.

So arise, warrior! Seize your destiny! The symphony of triumph awaits your resounding crescendo.

# Actionable Steps

**Acknowledge the Existence of Spiritual Antagonists**: Recognize that your journey to fulfill your purpose and maximize your potential may be met with opposition from unseen spiritual forces. Understand that your problems may have a spiritual origin and not simply be chance occurrences in the natural world.

**Engage in Spiritual Warfare through Prayer and Fasting**: Declare a period of focused prayer and fasting to actively combat the forces of darkness. Use prayer as a weapon, fervently seeking God's intervention and guidance. Combine prayer with increased efforts and determination in pursuing your goals and breakthroughs.

**Seek Divine Revelation and Spiritual Understanding**: As you engage in prayer and fasting, open yourself to receiving divine insights and understanding. Ask God to illuminate your spiritual perception and discern the necessary adjustments and actions you need to take to overcome obstacles.

**Persist in Prayer until Breakthrough**: Do not give up or leave the presence of God until you obtain your breakthrough. Maintain a posture of persistence, relying on the power of prayer and the presence of God to dismantle the spiritual hindrances in your path.

**Position Yourself in the Secret Place of the Most High**: Enter into a place of intimate prayer and communion with God. Seek His presence and abide under the protective shadow of the Almighty. Understand that in His presence, no power can withstand you, and darkness fades away.

**Embrace Spiritual Sight and Hearing**: Ask God to open the eyes of your spirit and the ears of your understanding. Seek to perceive and comprehend the spiritual realm beyond what ordinary senses can perceive. Develop a thirst for spiritual sight and hearing to discern the machinations at play in your life and to receive divine revelation.

**Claim Your Victory through the Power of God's Presence**: Recognize that the presence of God empowers you to reclaim what rightfully belongs to you. Stand firm in the authority and name of Jesus Christ, knowing that His name compels every knee to bow. Utilize His presence to overcome the obstacles and hindrances that have impeded your progress.

**March Forward**: Armed with the knowledge of spiritual warfare and the power of prayer, move forward on your journey with unwavering determination. Let the truth of God's Word be your guiding light, illuminating the path of victory. Embrace the mindset of a warrior, persisting in the face of challenges and defying the forces of darkness.

**Embrace Your Destiny**: Recognize that your purpose and destiny are waiting to be realized. Seize your destiny with courage and conviction, knowing that the victory has already been won in the name of Jesus Christ. March forward, confident in the triumph that awaits you.

**Stand United and Support Others**: Remember that you are not alone in the spiritual battle. Stand united with fellow believers, supporting and encouraging one another. Share the knowledge and revelations you have gained to empower others on their own journeys of fulfillment and purpose.

### *Medical Disclaimer:*

*Please note that the mention of fasting above is intended for spiritual and personal growth purposes and should not be interpreted as medical advice. Fasting can have potential health risks and may not be suitable for everyone. It is important to consult with a qualified healthcare professional before undertaking any fasting regimen, especially if you have underlying medical conditions, are taking medication, are pregnant or breastfeeding, or have a history of disordered eating. The information provided is not intended to diagnose, treat, cure, or prevent any disease. The responsibility lies with the individual to make informed decisions regarding their health and well-being.*

# CHAPTER 8

# The Waiting Room Chronicles
## Lessons in Patience

### The Agony of Waiting: When Time Seems to Stand Still

Picture yourself in a waiting room, filled with restlessness and impatience. The minutes stretch into hours, and frustration begins to seep into your soul. We have all experienced the agony of waiting in different spheres of life—the doctor's office, the beauty salon, the barber shop, or the mechanic's workshop. Life, too, has its own waiting rooms, where we yearn for divine intervention and hope for God to work wonders in our lives.

The waiting room of life is that sacred space where we realize the depths of our helplessness and the magnitude of God's power. It is when we come face to face with the stark reality that our situation is as dry and lifeless as the bones in Ezekiel's vision, and only the King of Kings can breathe life into them. Every soul that looks up to God, seeking His touch, finds themselves in this waiting room.

As I unexpectedly found myself in this waiting room, I had no inkling of how long my stay would be. The darkness seemed unending, with no glimmer of hope except for the light of Christ illuminating my path. I languished in the waiting room for years, and with each passing moment, new challenges emerged, amplifying the difficulties of my journey.

## The Battle Within: Overcoming Misery and Naysayers

In this waiting room, the weight of my past misery clung to me, clouding the vision of those around me. Yeses turned to nos, doors slammed shut, and the world seemed to conspire against me, deepening the wounds of yesteryear. I realized that another battle lay ahead, a steep ascent requiring divine intervention for me to overcome. Little did I know that this battle would set the stage for a transformative turn of events, forever altering the course of my life. But before we delve into these events, let us reflect on the purpose behind the waiting.

## Unveiling the Purpose: Lessons Learned in the Waiting Room

Why must we wait, often enduring what feels like an eternity? While I may not possess all the answers, I have come to understand that God uses the waiting room to mold and shape us. Though His providential power could answer our prayers in an instant, the lessons He desires to teach us can only be learned through the passage of time. These lessons become the building blocks of our wisdom, equipping us to help others along their journeys.

Consider a course curriculum, meticulously structured to ensure each chapter builds upon the previous one. Similarly, the waiting room of life is a vital chapter in our personal narrative, one that will prove invaluable in the future. It is within the confines of this waiting room that we gain firsthand experience that enables us to uplift and inspire others who find themselves in similar circumstances.

## The Agony and the Promise: Finding Solace Amid Despair

The waiting room is a painful place, rife with emotional turmoil. It is a realm of ups and downs, where depression, rejection, tears, scorn, and humiliation become familiar companions. In these moments, it may seem as though the world has turned against us. We knock on doors, yet no one seems to answer. We hold on to hope, only to be met with disappointment. We yearn for a resounding yes, only to be greeted by a chorus of nos. Our world crumbles before our eyes, leaving us feeling utterly helpless. At times, we question if God even cares. But, dear friend, know this—God cares deeply for you.

Although this may be an arduous season, if you maintain a pure heart and unwavering faith in God's purpose for your life, blessings will come knocking at your door. Within the waiting room, God is cultivating patience within you. James 1:3 reminds us that the trying of our faith produces patience, a virtue of immeasurable worth. Personally, I can attest to the fact that the adversities I have faced have infused me with a newfound patience in both the spiritual and material realms.

## Conclusion: The Tapestry Unveiled: The Masterful Work of God

In the chapters that follow, prepare to witness the magnificent workings of God in the kingdom of humans. Allow yourself to be captivated by the grandeur and intricacy of His divine tapestry. Though you may find yourself in the waiting room today, remember that this chapter of your life is purposeful and essential for your future. Embrace the lessons, endure the trials, and hold fast to your faith, for in due time, your waiting will bear fruit.

Stay blessed, dear reader, as you navigate the waiting room, knowing that God's masterpiece is being woven in the unseen realms.

# Actionable Steps

**Embrace the Waiting Room:** Recognize that the waiting room is a sacred space where you can experience personal growth and divine intervention. Embrace this season of waiting as an opportunity for God to work wonders in your life.

**Cultivate Patience:** Understand that waiting can be agonizing, but it also presents an opportunity to develop patience. Commit to cultivating patience in your life, both in the spiritual and material realms, knowing that it is a virtue of immeasurable worth.

**Seek Divine Guidance:** In moments of darkness and uncertainty, turn to God for guidance and strength. Trust in His purpose for your life and lean on Him for comfort and wisdom as you navigate the waiting room.

**Learn from the Lessons:** Be open to the lessons that the waiting room has to offer. Recognize that the challenges and experiences you encounter during this time are building blocks of wisdom that will equip you to uplift and inspire others on their own journeys.

**Maintain Faith:** Hold fast to your faith, even when it feels like the world has turned against you. Remember that God cares deeply for you and is working behind the scenes. Trust in His timing and believe that blessings will come knocking at your door as you remain steadfast in your faith.

**Endure with Hope**: While in the waiting room, it's important to maintain hope and not lose sight of the promises of God. Even in moments of despair and disappointment, hold on to the belief that God's plan for your life is unfolding and that blessings are on the horizon.

**Reflect and Encourage**: As you navigate your own waiting room, take time to reflect on your experiences and the lessons you've learned. Use your newfound wisdom to encourage and support others who may find themselves in similar circumstances. Share your journey and offer hope to those who are waiting.

**Trust the Unseen Work**: Understand that there is a masterful work being woven in the unseen realms of your life. Trust that God is orchestrating the events and circumstances to bring about His purpose for you. Have faith that in due time, the tapestry will be unveiled, revealing the magnificent workings of God in your life.

Remember, dear reader, that your waiting room is not in vain. Embrace the waiting, endure with patience, and trust in the divine plan. Stay blessed as you navigate this season, knowing that God is working all things together for your good.

# CHAPTER 9

# A Vision of Promise
## Embracing Divine Guidance

### A Rainy Night Vision: The Unveiling of a Prophetic Promise

During one of those uncertain years of my life, while I was sleeping, I found myself in the embrace of a vision. It was a rainy night, and in my dream, I walked along the curb of a private property. As I looked up, I saw a tall building with a name written boldly on it, the name of the institution where I would complete my medical residency training. Though the name was withheld from me, the Lord assured me it was a part of His grand plan.

### Waiting on God's Timing: Pieces of the Puzzle Unfold

In the realm of dreams, God revealed a glimpse of His purpose for my life, but He chose not to reveal every detail at once. Instead, He allowed the puzzle pieces to unfold gradually, beckoning me to depend on Him for guidance. Ecclesiastes 3:1 reminds us of the significance of time in God's divine plan. Every season has a purpose, and during the ugly season of uncertainty, God's vision assured me of His watchful eye and His unyielding plan for my life.

## Embracing God's Plans: Clinging to His Promises

Jeremiah 29:11 serves as a comforting reminder of God's good plans for His children. Despite setbacks and trials, God's intentions are never to harm us but to lead us into the fulfillment of His promises. However, to witness the manifestation of God's plans, we must hold firmly to His promises, undeterred by the cares of life. Like an athlete focused on the prize, we must keep our eyes fixed on the goal set before us.

## Answering the Divine Call: The Turning Point

Amid the wait for God's promise to materialize in my professional life, I encountered two life-altering visitations from the Lord. His voice resonated within me, emphasizing the call He had placed upon my life. It was a call I had sought confirmation for, and God made it clear that the path to abundance lay in heeding His call. Embracing His calling led to the birth of Jehiah Ministries (JHM), Inc., an endeavor that would bring God's liberation to those held captive by darkness.

## Decapitating the Kingdom of Darkness: Pursuing Purpose while Waiting

As I patiently waited for the fulfillment of God's promise, I realized that I could still wage war against the kingdom of darkness. Determined not to be hindered by Satan's tactics, I embraced the privilege of being used by God to set others free from bondage. The years that followed were marked by extraordinary movements of God through ministry, and I witnessed countless testimonies of God's deliverance and victories in the lives of those touched by His grace.

## Journey to the Promised Program: The Heavenly Interview

Having resolved to obey God's call, I set out on a mission to secure my future through a medical residency, one of the last stages in the process before one can become a medical doctor. Before my physical interview, the Lord took me on a heavenly journey in a vision. I traversed through states, passing colleges, until I reached the destination where the interview would take place. Little did I know that this spiritual journey had already sealed my fate, and the interview would unfold exactly as God had ordained.

## The Manifestation of Promise: Meharry Medical College

My interview at Meharry Medical College was nothing short of miraculous. God's hand was evident as He guided me to the very room I had seen in my vision. It was a surreal experience, solidifying my belief in the living God who orchestrates events in ways that surpass human comprehension. Months later, I received the long-awaited news of my acceptance into the program. The promise had been fulfilled, and I stood in awe of God's faithfulness.

## Living the Promise: Gratitude and Perseverance

Today, I stand as a fully licensed physician, living the promise God revealed to me through His vision. I offer my heartfelt gratitude to God for His grace and the strength He provided for me to weather the storms of life. I am indebted to those who believed in me, even when I struggled to believe in myself. The journey was not without its challenges, but through obedience and unwavering faith, I have witnessed the unfathomable wonders of God's plan unfolding in my life.

## Conclusion
### A Life Transformed: Embracing the Journey

In the chapters preceding this one, my story has unfolded as a testament to the transformative power of God's guidance. Each step, from the vision in the night to the fulfillment of promise, has shaped my character and deepened my faith. As you navigate your own journey, may this chapter serve as a reminder that God's promises are worth waiting for and that His plans are far greater than our own. Embrace the divine guidance that leads you to your purpose, and hold fast to the promises He has spoken over your life. The tapestry of your story is yet to be fully unveiled, and with God as the master weaver, it will be a work of unimaginable beauty.

## Actionable Steps

**Embrace Divine Guidance**: Reflect on the vision or calling that God has placed in your life. Acknowledge that God's plans may unfold gradually and that you must trust His timing and guidance.

**Seek Confirmation**: If you have doubts or uncertainties about the path God has set before you, seek confirmation through prayer, meditation, and wise counsel from trusted individuals in your life.

**Hold Firmly to God's Promises**: In times of waiting and uncertainty, cling to God's promises as revealed in Scripture. Remind yourself of Jeremiah 29:11 and other verses that affirm God's good plans for your life. Write down these promises and refer to them regularly to strengthen your faith.

**Answer the Divine Call**: If you sense a specific calling from God, respond with obedience and a willingness to follow His lead. Be open to the ways in which God may use you to bring about His purposes and make a positive impact in others' lives.

**Seek God's Presence and Guidance Daily**: Develop a consistent practice of spending time in prayer, meditation, and reading Scripture to seek God's presence and guidance each day. Cultivate a personal relationship with God and invite Him to direct your steps, reveal His plans, and provide wisdom and discernment. This intentional connection with God will deepen your trust in Him and enable you to navigate the twists and turns of your journey with confidence and clarity.

**Pursue Your Purpose**: Take practical steps toward fulfilling your purpose. Whether it's seeking further education, starting a ministry, or pursuing a career, align your actions with the calling and vision God has placed in your heart.

**Trust in Divine Guidance:** Trust that God is intricately involved in every aspect of your journey. Rely on His guidance, even when it comes to the smallest details, knowing that He is faithful to orchestrate events and open doors according to His perfect plan.

**Express Gratitude and Practice Perseverance:** Cultivate a heart of gratitude for God's faithfulness throughout your journey. Give thanks for the challenges and victories, as they have shaped you and deepened your faith. Persevere in times of difficulty, holding on to your trust in God's promises and His ability to fulfill them.

**Share Your Story:** As your journey unfolds and God's promises are fulfilled, share your testimony with others. Be a source of encouragement and inspiration to those who are still waiting for their own promises to manifest. Offer support and hope to those who may be facing similar challenges.

**Embrace the Unfolding Journey:** Recognize that your life is a work in progress, and the tapestry of your story is yet to be fully unveiled. Embrace the ongoing process of growth, transformation, and divine guidance, knowing that God's plans for your life are far greater than anything you can imagine.

May you find strength, purpose, and joy as you embrace divine guidance and walk in the fulfillment of God's promises for your life. Trust in His faithfulness and allow Him to lead you on a journey of profound impact and purpose.

# CHAPTER 10

# Transitioning from the Known to the Unknown

## Embracing God's Equation for Success

### The Equation of Revelation: Illuminating Paths in the Darkness

Imagine yourself standing at the edge of a vast, uncharted territory, shrouded in darkness. In your hands, you hold an equation, where $x$ represents the known, $y$ the unknown, and $z$ the answer you seek. But there is a crucial element missing—a divine light to guide your way. God, the radiant constant, beckons you to include Him in your equation, illuminating the path that leads from uncertainty to certainty. When His presence is absent, your search for answers will continue without resolution. God declares, "I am who I am! I am constant! I am the Lord. I change not!"

## Embracing Divine Direction: The Unsettling Nudge toward Uncharted Horizons

Close your eyes and envision a stirring within your spirit—an unrelenting nudge, urging you to venture beyond your comfort zone. You find yourself in a vast wilderness, filled with towering mountains and winding paths. In this moment of unsettledness, God invites you to grasp His hand and allow Him to lead you through the wilderness of uncertainty. He wants to transform your restlessness into a compass that points toward the promised land of certainty. Remember, His thoughts toward you are good and not evil; He longs to grant you an expected end (Jeremiah 29:11). Will you choose to follow His divine direction?

## Seeking God's Voice: The Symphony of Divine Whispers

Imagine stepping into a sacred sanctuary, a hallowed space where the divine and the human intertwine. Here, within a symphony of silence, you are attuned to the delicate whispers of God's voice. Thirsting for Him, you immerse yourself in His Word and devote time to prayer, creating a channel of divine communication. Holiness becomes the frequency through which His voice resonates. "Blessed are they which hunger and thirst after righteousness, for they shall be filled" (Matthew 5:6). As you draw nearer to God, His voice becomes a familiar melody, guiding you in the harmonious dance of life.

## Embracing God's Timing: The Tapestry of Patience Unfolds

Envision a vast tapestry unfurling before your eyes, a masterpiece intricately woven with threads of waiting and patience. God's timing, like a skilled weaver, adds depth and beauty to the fabric of your life. Sometimes, He weaves in silence, prompting you to exercise patience as He orchestrates the symphony of your existence behind the scenes. In these moments, surrendering to His will births patience within you. Waiting upon the Lord grants renewal of strength, equipping you to soar high on wings like eagles. He prepares you to conquer mountains and obstacles, ensuring that weariness and fatigue do not overtake you. Through waiting, character is forged that can withstand the tests of time and trials.

## The Power of Prayer: The Fiery Embrace of Divine Conversation

Visualize a roaring fire, its flames dancing and crackling with intensity. Prayer, like the oxygen that fuels this fire, sustains and invigorates the soul. It is the language through which you commune with your heavenly Father, a divine conversation that breathes life into every aspect of your being. In the place of prayer, victories are won, and transformation occurs. Release the burdens of your heart through fervent prayer, and watch as God fights on your behalf. He becomes your advocate when you have no voice, raising "destiny helpers" when you find yourself helpless and alone. Prayer, your most powerful weapon, holds the key to unlocking God's abundant blessings.

## Final Reflections

### *Embracing God's Faithfulness: A Tapestry Woven with Divine Threads*

Picture a vibrant tapestry, woven with threads of faithfulness, hard work, and perseverance. This masterpiece of God's faithfulness unfolds in the lives of those who cultivate a close relationship with Jesus Christ. As we approach the conclusion of this book, let the testimonies of His intervention and goodness resonate within your heart. His invitation stands: If you have not taken your commitment to Christ seriously, I implore you to join me in recommitting your life to Him. And if you have never known Him, I extend an invitation to taste and see His goodness and mercy. He is the one who can truly change your life.

# A Prayer of Commitment to Jesus Christ

As we reach the end of this journey, let us bow our heads and utter a prayer of surrender:

"Lord Jesus Christ, I stand in awe of Your glory and grace. I confess that You are the Son of God, who came to earth and died for my sins, offering me the gift of everlasting life. I humbly ask for Your forgiveness and surrender my life to You. You are my Lord and Savior, and I commit to serving You all the days of my life. Use me for Your glory and guide me along the path of certainty. Amen."

*Date:*

_____

*My commitment prayer:*

_____

_____

_____

_____

_____

_____

_____

_____

May you carry the lessons learned within the pages of this book as you embrace God's equation for success. As you step into the unknown, may vivid imagery and captivating tales of faithfulness inspire you to incorporate God as the constant in your life's equation. Trust in His divine direction, seek His voice, embrace patience, and wield the power of prayer. Above all, may you experience the profound transformation that comes from a close relationship with Jesus Christ, the source of all life's great wonders.

## Actionable Steps

**Make God the Constant in Your Equation**: Recognize the importance of including God in every equation you must solve in this life. Invite Him to guide you through uncertainty, and seek His wisdom as you navigate the unknown. Dedicate time each day to acknowledging His presence and surrendering your plans to His divine guidance.

**Step Out of Your Comfort Zone**: Embrace the unsettling nudge within your spirit that urges you to venture beyond the familiar. Take courageous steps outside of your comfort zone, trusting that God is leading you toward the promised land of certainty. Allow Him to transform your restlessness into a compass that points you in the right direction.

**Cultivate a Channel of Divine Communication**: Create a sacred space for seeking God's voice. Immerse yourself in His Word, spend dedicated time in prayer, and listen for His whispers. Hunger and thirst after righteousness, inviting God to speak to you and reveal His plans. Develop a habit of actively listening and discerning His guidance.

**Embrace Patience and God's Timing**: Understand that God's timing is perfect. Embrace patience as He weaves together the tapestry of your life. Surrender your own plans and desires, trusting that His timing is better than your own. Seek strength in waiting upon the Lord, knowing that He will renew your energy and equip you for the challenges ahead.

**Harness the Power of Prayer**: Engage in fervent and consistent prayer, inviting God into every aspect of your life. Approach prayer as a fiery embrace of divine conversation, releasing your burdens and seeking God's intervention. Trust that through prayer, God fights on your behalf, opens doors, and brings forth His blessings and favor.

**Recommit Your Life to Christ**: If you have not taken your commitment to Christ seriously or if you have never known Him, consider recommitting your life to Him. Acknowledge Jesus Christ as your Lord and Savior, seeking forgiveness for your sins and surrendering your life to His guidance. Cultivate a close relationship with Him, allowing His faithfulness to be woven into the tapestry of your life.

## Closing Prayer

"Lord Jesus Christ, I surrender my life to You. I invite You to be the constant in my life's equation. Guide me through uncertainty and illuminate my path with Your divine light. Give me the courage to step out of my comfort zone and follow Your divine direction. Help me to cultivate a channel of communication with You, seeking Your voice and wisdom. Grant me patience as I trust in Your perfect timing. I harness the power of prayer, inviting You into every aspect of my life. I recommit my life to You, Lord, and I invite You to transform me from the inside out. In Your name, I pray. Amen."

May these actionable steps empower you to embrace God's equation for success, trusting in His guidance and experiencing His transformative power in your life.

---

---

---

---

---

---

---

---

# Acknowledgments

I am deeply grateful to the extraordinary individuals who have played pivotal roles in the creation of this book. To my cherished family, friends, and mentors, your unwavering support and valuable contributions in reviewing this manuscript have been instrumental in shaping its essence. At various stages of my journey, you have been vessels through which guidance, both divine and earthly, has flowed, and I am profoundly thankful for your presence in my life.

*I want to extend my deepest gratitude to my Heavenly Father, the source of all wisdom, love, and guidance. Throughout my journey, You have been my constant companion, illuminating the path before me and leading me towards a life of purpose and fulfillment. Your unwavering presence and divine orchestration have shaped every chapter of my story, unveiling my authentic self and guiding me towards personal growth. Your grace has been my strength in times of uncertainty, and Your faithfulness has never wavered. I am humbled by Your love and grateful for the countless blessings You have bestowed upon me. Thank You, Heavenly Father, for being the ultimate author of my life's narrative and for filling each page with Your wisdom, grace, and goodness. To You, I offer my heartfelt appreciation and dedicate the unfolding chapters of my life to bringing glory to Your name. Amen.*

To my beloved wife, Dr. Waire Oyewole, you have been my rock and guiding light in the fight of destiny. Your unwavering support and strength have carried me through the trials and tribulations on this path. Without your steadfast commitment, I would not have conquered the challenges I encountered. Your love and belief in me have been a beacon of hope, and for that, I am eternally grateful.

Jehiah, Abraham, and Elizabeth, my dear children, your unwavering faith and commitment to our family's journey have been awe-inspiring. Thank you for standing strong and enduring the hardships of those trying years with patience and fortitude. Your presence and contributions have woven themselves into the very tapestry of this story, leaving an indelible mark that words cannot fully capture.

Apostle Akin Oyewole, my father, I extend my heartfelt appreciation for being an exceptional role model in my life. From the earliest days of my existence, you guided me onto the path of life, instilling within me an unwavering belief in myself and in a higher power. Your mentorship throughout my childhood and into adulthood has shaped the very core of my being. I am grateful for the profound wisdom you have imparted to me.

Pastor (Mrs) Moji Oyewole, my mother, I am forever thankful for your tutelage during my formative years. You taught me the importance of fasting, praying, and waiting upon a power greater than ourselves. These simple yet profound lessons have formed the bedrock of the successes highlighted in this book. Your love and dedication as a mother have touched my heart, and I am eternally grateful.

To Mrs. Mayowa Oyewole-obogbeni and Mr. Gbenga Oyewole, my dear brother and sister, I am immensely grateful for your unwavering support and the time you dedicated to reviewing the manuscript and providing invaluable input. Your encouragement has uplifted my spirits, and I deeply appreciate your steadfast commitment to my journey.

Prophetess Yetunde Sadoh, your mentorship has been a divine source of inspiration. Through your teachings, you have consistently reinforced my trust in a higher power. The messages you have conveyed as a vessel of divine guidance have impacted my life in profound ways. I am grateful for your selflessness and the transformative influence you have had on my spiritual growth.

Dr. Bola Ayodeji, Mr. Wola Ayodeji, Mr. and Mrs. Akinretoye, your unwavering support throughout the years has been a source of encouragement that transcends words. Your presence in my life, particularly during my early days in the United States, laid the essential foundation for my journey in this new land. Your belief in me has propelled me forward, and I am forever grateful.

Dr. Tola Emmanuel and Dr. Ronke Adekunle-Adetokun, as trusted friends, I extend my deepest gratitude for your insightful review of the manuscript. Your invaluable input has enriched the content and elevated its impact. Your friendship and unwavering support have been a source of strength throughout this process.

Dr. Millard Collins, Late Dr. Medhat Kalliny, and Ms. Stephanie Glenn, I am profoundly thankful for your unwavering belief in me. I firmly believe that divine orchestration placed you at Meharry Medical College, making you instrumental in the grand scheme of things. Your unwavering support and faith in my abilities have played an integral role in shaping this journey.

To my publisher, editor, and designer, I extend my heartfelt appreciation for your invaluable assistance. Your expertise, dedication, and collaborative effort have transformed this manuscript into a tangible work of art. I am grateful for the collective passion and commitment that have brought this book to fruition.

To all those whose names may not be mentioned here, yet have provided support, prayers, and encouragement along the way, I am deeply thankful. Your belief in me has been a driving force, and I am forever indebted to your contributions.

Finally, to the readers of this book, I extend my deepest gratitude. It is my earnest hope that the words within these pages resonate with your hearts, ignite transformation, and awaken a renewed sense of hope and purpose in your lives. May this journey together be one of growth, inspiration, and profound empowerment.

With profound appreciation,

**Dr. Dotun Oyewole**

Contact Dr. Dotun Oyewole at **PhosPublishing@gmail.com**

# About the Author

Dr. Oyewole is a father, husband, Bible teacher, Christian minister, author, motivational speaker, entrepreneur, and physician. With a Doctor of Medicine (MD) degree and a notable track record of leadership and accomplishments in family medicine, his expertise extends far beyond the realm of healing bodies—it delves into guiding souls toward self-discovery and purpose.

In 2013, Dr. Oyewole founded Jehiah Ministries (JIIM), Inc., a ministry renowned for its fervent intercessory prayer and unwavering commitment to sharing the unfiltered word of God. Through his passionate delivery of scripture, coupled with a remarkable ability to ignite the fire of prayer within others, he has breathed new life into countless souls and become a beacon of hope. His mission is to help individuals tap into their hidden potential and experience true freedom in every facet of their lives.

Beyond his spiritual calling, Dr. Oyewole possesses an exceptional gift—a unique lens through which he captures the essence of captivating moments, not as a traditional photographer, but as a masterful storyteller. His words paint vivid imagery, transporting listeners into transformative experiences that linger long after the last page is turned or the final sentence spoken. With each interaction, Dr. Oyewole invites his audience into a world where profound insights and heartfelt wisdom intertwine.

Residing in the vibrant landscape of Tennessee alongside his wife, Dr. Waire Oyewole, and their three beautiful children, Dr. Oyewole's dedication to service and unwavering devotion to God's teachings have positioned him as a transformative force in the lives of those he encounters.

## Leave a Review!

For a self-published author like myself, reviews mean the world! Please write an honest review on the platform from which you purchased this book. I read every one!